CALIGULA
THE THIRD EMPEROR

THE HISTORY HOUR

Copyright © 2018 by Kolme Korkeudet Oy

All rights reserved.

No part of this book may be reproduced in any form or by any electronic or mechanical means, including information storage and retrieval systems, without written permission from the author, except for the use of brief quotations in a book review.

CONTENTS

PART I
Introduction 1

PART II
THE FIRST DYNASTY OF ROME
Caligula 5
Son of a Warrior 11

PART III
THE NEW EMPEROR TAKES THE THRONE
Auspicious Beginnings 23

PART IV
A CHANGED MAN
The New Caligula 29
Bloodshed and Brutality 33
Plots and Schemes 41

PART V
A VERY UN-ROMAN EMPEROR
A Hellenistic Education 45
Enough Is Enough 47
Aftermath 51

PART VI
IT'S ALL TRUE...OR IS IT?
Contradictions and Inconsistencies 55
Poison Pens 61

PART VII
LESSONS TO LEARN
Believe It or Not, He Had Good Qualities 67
Famous for Bad Behavior 70
Lessons to Be Learned 73

Afterword	77
Additional Reading	79
Your Free eBook!	81

❧ I ❦
INTRODUCTION

☙❧

Caesar cannot be a fool!
 Caligula

☙❧

There are certain people in history whose names are remembered the world over long after their deaths. Some are known for their bravery and excellence, like Nelson Mandela or Leonardo da Vinci. Others are known not because of the good they did, but because their barbarity and crimes are too terrible to be forgotten.

☙❧

The name Caligula has come down to us in the modern world

as one of these terrible people. His name is instantly associated with madness and cruelty. Roman historians, some virtually his contemporaries, listed him as one of the worst emperors that Rome ever had. He has been portrayed in ancient sources as tyrannical, sexually deviant, cruel, and given to the sort of personal and financial excesses that would make even Marie Antoinette blush.

※

First, we will examine the stories as they've come to us from historians like Suetonius, Cassius Dio and Tacitus. Then we'll examine a new interpretation of the same evidence put forward by German historian Aloys Winterling.

※

Caligula is infamous. Perhaps that infamy is not deserved.

II
THE FIRST DYNASTY OF ROME

※

I have existed from the morning of the world and I shall exist until the last star falls from the night. Although I have taken the form of Gaius Caligula, I am all men as I am no man and therefore I am a God.
Caligula

CALIGULA

༺༻

The first dynasty in the history of the Roman Empire was the Julio-Claudian dynasty, which ruled Rome from the death of Augustus in 27 BC until the last member of the dynasty, Nero, committed suicide in AD 68. The emperors in this family line have been described as mad, bad, and dangerous to know. Before we get to the particulars of Caligula's own story, we need to lay a little ground work.

༺༻

ROMAN SOCIETY WAS SET up along rigidly hierarchical lines. The main groups of people were patricians, plebeians, proles and non-citizens (women, children, foreigners, freedmen and slaves). Within the first two groups, there were additional divisions based upon wealth. Roman social standing, especially in the time of Caligula, was based almost entirely upon the riches that a man had and displayed. Proles were the landless poor, people who were free-born and therefore citizens, but who were too poor to buy their way into the social strata above them. Plebeians were the average citizens of the Roman world, and patricians were the noble families who traced their lineage to the men who formed the first Senate after the city of Rome was founded.

※

THE PLEBIAN CLASS was divided up into five groupings, fifth being the lowest and first being highest. Each division was responsible for supplying its own weapons and armor when they were called to serve in the army, but the required equipment was scaled according to the man's wealth. The lowest plebian rank, the fifth rank, was made up of men who had between 11,000 and 12,500 as (a bronze roman coin, the lowest valued coin in circulation that was worth one-quarter of a sestertius) and they were required only to provide slings or javelins. The highest plebian rank was anyone with 100,000 as or above, and they were required to provide a helm, a round shield, a cuirass (a piece of armor made up of a back plate and a breast plate fastened together with leather straps), greaves (armored shin guards), sword and spear.

※

THE PATRICIAN CLASS was made up of *equites* (knights, or the equestrian class) and the *senatores*. The equestrian class was available to plebeians if they could afford to buy their way in (at a cost of 400,000 sesterces), but the *senatores* were an elite group made up only of men who had either been elected to the Senate by winning the post of *quaestor* or who had been appointed to the Senate by the emperor.

※

THERE WAS a strict path that men in the *senatores* class pursued in the rush for personal power. This was called the *cursus honorum*, and it began with an elected position called *quaestor*. The *quaestor* was one of twenty men who were responsible for the financial administration of the empire, including acting as paymaster for the army. The minimum age was 30, although patricians were allowed to stand for the office at the age of 28. The position was held for a term of one year. The next step on the *cursus* was the *aedile*. There were two patrician *aediles* and two plebian *aediles*. These officials supervised public works and the upkeep of temples and other public buildings. They were also responsible for organizing gladiatorial games for the public to view. The minimum age for an *aedile* was 36. At 39, a man could take on the next role in the *cursus*, the *praetor*. *Praetors* sat as judges at trials and had the right to grant court orders and dispensations. The most prestigious posts in this rank were the *praetor peregrinus*, the chief justice in all cases involving foreigners, and the *praetor urbanus,* the chief justice of Rome.

※

THE NEXT STEP WAS *CONSUL*. There were two consuls at any given time, and they were extremely powerful men. They were the supreme commanders of the Roman army, each man personally commanding two legions, or two thousand troops. They were granted twelve bodyguards called *lictors*, who were responsible for executing sentences on the convicted and for carrying the *fasces*, a totem of office that accompanied the consul everywhere he went. The consuls were the only men in Rome who were allowed to wear a purple stripe on their togas (the *toga praetexta*), maroon shoes and a gold signet ring showing the face of the emperor.

⁂

THE RANKINGS GIVEN ABOVE ARE important to keep in mind as we continue through the story of Caligula. Under his rule, rank was a very important consideration, as we will see.

⁂

THE NAME of the dynasty comes from the two main branches of the Imperial family, *gens Julia* and *gens Claudia*. A *gens* was a family with the same name (*nomen*) claiming descent from a common ancestor, usually someone with consular status or above. A *gens* is similar to the surnames that we use today. The family in the *gens Julia* claimed descent from Gaius Julius Iulus, who was a consul of Rome in 489 BC. The *gens Claudia* descended from consul Appius Claudius Sabinus Regillensus, who held his position from 495 BC. These were solidly patrician families whose grip on power had been solidified long before Julius Caesar became dictator of Rome. It was his great-nephew and adopted son, Gaius Julius Caesar Octavianus, later known as Augustus Caesar, who was the first Roman emperor. When Augustus was acclaimed emperor by the Senate, the Julio-Claudians became the de facto royal family.

⁂

INTERESTINGLY, the practice of primogeniture, when the right of succession passes to the first-born child, was not actually a feature of the Julio-Claudian dynasty. There were five emperors in the dynasty, and all of them were adopted by the men who ruled before him.

※

THE FIRST EMPEROR of the dynasty was Tiberius Caesar Augustus. He was born into *gens Claudia* but took the Julian name after his mother, Livia Drusilla, married Emperor Augustus. Tiberius eventually married Augustus's daughter, Julia the Elder, thereby securing his position in the Julian family as well as his place in line for the throne. Tiberius only sired one child, a son named Drusus Julius Caesar. He had no children with Julia the Elder.

※

AT THE URGING of the Emperor Augustus, Tiberius adopted his nephew Germanicus Julius Caesar, who was the son of the able general Nero Claudius Drusus and Antonia Minor, the daughter of Marc Antony and Octavia Minor, who was Emperor Augustus's sister. Tiberius did not want to adopt Germanicus, but the Emperor (who would have preferred Germanicus to Tiberius as his heir) made the adoption a condition for Tiberius's accession.

※

GERMANICUS WAS MARRIED to Agrippina the Elder, who was Augustus's granddaughter and a formidable person in her own right. She was brave and unusually forthright and public for a Roman matron in a time when Roman women were expected to be quiet and demure. The average Roman woman rarely left her family home. Agrippina the Elder went with Germanicus to the camps of the army, and she was at his side during many of his campaigns. The couple had nine children, two of whom died as infants and one who passed away from fever in early childhood. Of their surviving children, their third oldest son was named Gaius Julius Caesar Augustus Germanicus. History knows him as Caligula.

SON OF A WARRIOR

❦

Germanicus would have been a good emperor, had he survived. He was intelligent, charming, handsome, generous, ambitious within reason, and he had a clear understanding of royal and civic duty. His career began when he ascended to the rank of *quaestor* before he had even reached the age of majority. The *quaestor* was theoretically an elected position, but given his family ties, one could be pardoned for wondering exactly how free and fair Germanicus's election actually was.

❦

UNLIKE MANY WHO came before him, and especially unlike other members of his family, Germanicus was beloved by the people. He went on to become proconsul of Germania Inferior, and he commanded fully one-third of the Roman army in successful campaigns against the Germanic tribes. His name, Germanicus, was first given to his own father as recognition for successful warfare against these same tribes, and the glory attendant to the name was passed to little Gaius, who was expected to follow the family tradition of military victory.

When Gaius was two years old, he and his mother, Agrippina the Elder, visited Germanicus at the front. The child was instantly the darling of the men, and his mere presence was known to quell riotous dissent within the ranks. The name Caligula means "Little Boots," and it was bestowed upon him with no small affection by the men under his father's command due to his mother's preference for dressing the boy in child-sized armor and regalia. Although the name was meant well and was a token of the love of the soldiers, he hated it, and when he became emperor, no one would dare to call him "Caligula" to his face.

Germanicus took command of the legions in Germania in AD 13 when those legions were in mutiny over unpaid wages and bonuses. Germanicus, without either orders or permission from Rome, took his soldiers on a devastating raid through the province. He paid all eight legions out of his own pocket and allowed them to sack and plunder Germania to make up for any real or perceived pecuniary shortfalls they had experienced under Tiberius's neglect. The raids were so successful that Germanicus and his legions spent the next three years plundering the German tribes, sending riches and honors back to Rome.

THE CAMPAIGN WAS BRUTAL. Germanicus thought that the eradication of the German tribes was the true goal of the fight, and the carnage was unspeakable. Through it all, Caligula, his mother and his siblings were at their father's side. It is possible that seeing such horrors at such a young age set the scene for Caligula's later mental illness.

※

HIS POPULARITY BEGAN to eclipse that of his uncle and adopted father. Emperor Tiberius was hugely unpopular with the masses because of his refusal to properly attend to the business of state, his seemingly single-minded need to break every one of Augustus's promises, and whispers of sexual perversity. Jealousy sprang into the heart of the emperor, and while he was on campaign in Antioch, Germanicus suddenly and mysteriously died. He confessed to his wife on his deathbed that he suspected he had been poisoned by Tiberius, probably through the agency of the provincial governor Gnaeus Calpurnius Piso. Piso had long been Germanicus's rival and may or may not have been acting on Tiberius's behalf to undermine Germanicus's orders in Syria.

※

AGRIPPINA WAS NOT the sort of woman who took the death of her beloved husband quietly, or even well. She immediately began to loudly accuse Tiberius and Piso of Germanicus's murder. The public outcry that followed forced Tiberius's hand, and he summoned Piso to Rome to be tried by the Senate. Despite a spirited defense, Piso was convicted, and he chose to commit suicide rather than be sentenced. He never implicated Tiberius in the plot.

The accusations against Tiberius were already in motion, though, and Agrippina was loud with her complaints. She began to gather powerful friends, and she took part in a conspiracy against the emperor and his favorite, the Praetorian prefect Lucius Aelius Sejanus. The prefect was a brutal man, and when Tiberius abandoned Rome in favor of the island of Capri, Sejanus was left as de facto ruler. He was powerful and ambitious, and he steadily usurped the emperor's power. He recognized Agrippina and her children as a threat to his imperial ambitions, and he betrayed her to Tiberius. The emperor responded with charges of treason against her and her sons Nero and Drusus. The three were sent into exile on different islands, where they were subjected to brutality and starvation. Agrippina was flogged so viciously by her captors that she lost an eye. Ultimately, they all perished due to malnutrition, with Drusus said to have gone so mad with hunger that he tried to eat the stuffing out of his prison mattress.

Caligula and his younger sisters were somehow spared from Tiberius's wrath. This might have been because their father's popularity with the people and the army had been transferred to them. Unfortunately, as much as the children were loved by the common man, they were seen as obstacles by the patricians. As the last remaining son of the beloved Germanicus, Caligula was the focus of many senators' plots.

Plotting and scheming was rife in the Senate, and there

were dozens of allegations of treason that were made by one senator against another. Tiberius was paranoid by nature, and the more people came forward with accusations, the worse his paranoia became. He ordered huge numbers of arrests on the basis of scurrilous accusations, and he filled the prisons with people who had been betrayed by ambitious peers. Anything could be and was considered treason, ranging from actual plots against the emperor to complaints about his decisions. Any disparaging comment made against Tiberius was grounds for conviction, and often these convictions led to executions. People were afraid, never knowing if or when they would be accused, or by whom.

SEJANUS, the Praetorian to whom Tiberius left the management of his empire, began to have designs upon the throne. Drusus Julius Caesar, Tiberius's son, became the focus of Sejanus's scheming. He seduced Drusus's wife, Livilla, and with her assistance, he murdered Drusus by a slow application of poison. He asked for permission to marry Livilla, thereby gaining membership in the royal family, but the request was denied.

WITH STOLEN power in his hands, Sejanus assigned the Praetorian guard to carry Tiberius's correspondence from Capri to Rome. This gave Sejanus the opportunity to read and intercept any messages that were not in his best interests, and to gain the upper hand and advance knowledge of the wishes of the emperor.

SEJANUS ALSO POSITIONED the Praetorians to be more than just bodyguards to the emperor. They became a police force that could not be opposed, and they oppressed the people of Rome. The prefect was virtually the dictator of Rome, and Tiberius allowed it out of ignorance.

༄༅༅

SOON SEJANUS BECAME SO ENAMORED of his power that he became incautious. He began to enact purges against senators who opposed him, gaining the enmity of those senators who remained. News of Sejanus's excessive ambition was brought to Tiberius by his sister-in-law's slave who had earned a great deal of the emperor's trust. When he heard of the betrayal, Tiberius replaced Sejanus as prefect with a man named Quintus Naevius Macro. He then sent a letter to the Senate and asked for it to be read in the present of Sejanus.

༄༅༅

SEJANUS WAS SUMMONED to the Senate, and he believed that he was about to receive new honors. Unfortunately, what he received was a death sentence. The letter from Tiberius outlined his plots and misdeeds and demanded that Sejanus be executed on the spot. He was strangled to death in the Senate chambers and his body was thrown to the people, who tore it to pieces.

༄༅༅

IT WAS AT THIS TIME, following the demise of his mother and brothers, that Caligula was brought to Capri to live as Tiberius's ward. The young man was essentially a hostage, being kept close to Tiberius to prevent him from fomenting rebellions and conspiracies. Some whispers indicated that Caligula's good fortune was due to an unwholesome interest that Tiberius had for the comely boy. What happened there in Capri was never fully disclosed, but the gossip in the capital was lurid. For whatever reason, after spending most of his childhood under house arrest in the homes of various female relatives, Caligula was taken to Tiberius's personal retreat on the island of Capri.

※

CALIGULA AND TIBERIUS learned to loathe and distrust one another, but to the emperor's face, Caligula was unfailingly pleasant and obedient, concealing his distaste for the man who had destroyed his family. He was careful to never say anything critical of Tiberius, and even when others tried to draw him into their plots, he refused to become involved. He was shrewd, and he was gaining a reputation for cruelty and viciousness. He was said to enjoy watching the punishment of prisoners and slaves, and would have people tortured in front of him for his amusement. According to the Roman historian Suetonius, Tiberius said his reason for leaving Caligula alive was

> "that Caius (sic) was destined to be the ruin of himself and all mankind; and that he was rearing a hydra for the people of Rome, and a Phaeton for all the world."

The hatred between them was such that Caligula even brought a knife into Tiberius's bedroom with the intention of killing the emperor, but at the last moment he had a change of heart and flung the knife to the floor. Tiberius was too afraid of Caligula by this time to act on the attack, and the boy was never punished or even accused.

※

CALIGULA'S bizarre personal tastes began to show themselves at this time. He reportedly spent time at brothels and rough taverns while wearing a wig as a disguise. He was passionately devoted to theater and fancied himself a talented writer, and any comments to contrary would cause him to fly into a rage. He had incestuous affairs with his sisters, and was caught in the act by his grandmother Antonia. These early traits did not bode well for the future.

※

WHILE IN CAPRI, apart from whatever else was happening, young Caligula learned how to play the political game of currying favor through gifts and flattery. He gained in personal popularity while Tiberius' standing continued to decline.

※

IN THE YEAR 33, at the age of 21, Caligula married Junia Claudilla, daughter of a high-ranking aristocrat named Marcus Silanus. Junia died in childbirth the next year. Caligula then entered into an adulterous relationship with Ennia Naevia, the wife of Naevius Sutorius Macro, the prefect of the Praetorian guards. Caligula promised to marry her should he become emperor. In return, she convinced her powerful husband to support Caligula, and the two men became fast friends. Macro, who had Tiberius' ear, was probably the reason that the emperor named Caligula and his own grandson Tiberius Gemellus as co-heirs to the throne.

※

IN 37 AD, Caligula conspired with Macro to end the old emperor's life. They poisoned Tiberius, and while the old man lay on his death bed, Caligula tried to take the imperial ring from his finger. Tiberius held on tight, though, and either Caligula or Macro smothered the emperor with a pillow. According to Suetonius, one of Tiberius's servants witnessed the murder and tried to raise an alarm, but he was apprehended and crucified for his trouble.

※

CALIGULA WAS EMPEROR, and Rome would never be the same.

III
THE NEW EMPEROR TAKES THE THRONE

Let them hate me, so long as they fear me!
Caligula

Tiberius's will stipulated that the empire was to be ruled by Caligula and Tiberius Gemellus. The Senate, influenced by the still-shining popularity of Germanicus and with the instigation of Praetorian Prefect Macro, agreed to nullify Tiberius's will on the grounds that the late emperor had been insane. Gemellus came of age after he was stripped of his inheritance, and after the ceremony in which he was formally granted the toga of manhood (a rite of passage in Roman society), Caligula adopted Gemellus as his son and heir. As a consolation prize, Gemellus was named *princeps iuventutis*, or Prince of the Youth.

AUSPICIOUS BEGINNINGS

※

For the first six months of his reign, Caligula was prudent and stable. He buried Tiberius with all the trappings an emperor should have, despite his personal feelings for the man. He then went to Pandataria and the Pontian Islands to retrieve the ashes of his mother and brothers. He personally interred them in the Mausoleum of Augustus, then offered Circensian games in memory of his mother. He publicly burned the records of his family's treason trials, making a great show of not reading them and therefore not knowing who had betrayed his kin. He did, however, unbeknownst to most people, retain copies of every document that he so showily destroyed.

※

WHERE TIBERIUS HAD BEEN A LARGELY absent emperor with more disdain than care for the common people, Caligula restored voting rights, distributed bread and gifts, and hosted games and theatricals for the people's entertainment. He also ordered repairs to the temples and built two aqueducts, the Aqua Claudia and Anio Novus, both of which remain standing to this day. He paid all of Tiberius's debts and bequests, as well as those of Livia Augusta, Augustus's wife, whose will had previously been nullified. He restored vassal kings to their thrones and allowed them to collect back taxes for the years they had been deposed. His generosity also extended to the provinces, where he put on games and theatricals in Syracuse, Sicily and Gaul.

※

IN ROME ITSELF, he began a program to compensate people who lost property in fires. He pardoned all of the condemned and exiled men and women who had fallen on hard times due to Tiberius's paranoia, and he called them back to Rome. He annulled unpopular taxes and gave magistrates the right to make decisions without consulting him. He was everything the people believed that the son of Germanicus should be.

※

SUETONIUS WROTE,

> "Gaius (Caligula) himself tried to rouse men's devotion by courting popularity in every way."

Largely, he was successful. The people remembered their adoration of his father Germanicus, and their delight at having an emperor who wasn't Tiberius helped extend the honeymoon feelings. Wisely, knowing the power of the army in general and the Praetorian guard in particular, Caligula awarded huge cash bonuses and shortened enlistment periods for the army, something that had been a cause of unrest and even mutiny under Tiberius. He greatly rewarded the Praetorian Guard, especially its powerful prefect, Macro, who was seen as the power behind the throne.

※

IN THE EARLY days of his reign, Caligula was the very image of a good and benevolent ruler, but it was not to last. To quote Suetonius: "So much for Caligula as emperor; we must now tell of his career as a monster."

❧ IV ☙
A CHANGED MAN

৩✺৩

I don't care if they respect me so long as they fear me.
Caligula

৩✺৩

In October of 37 AD, Caligula fell desperately ill. He was so near death that the people mobbed the temples, making offerings and vows to the gods in hopes of saving the young emperor's life. No one knows the true nature of his affliction, and the ancient sources are mute as to his symptomatology. At the very least he suffered an extremely high fever and delirium, possibly with seizures. Some have speculated that he had encephalopathy, or a swelling of the brain. Others believe that he suffered from epilepsy. Whatever the illness was, it changed him, and he emerged from his sick bed as a very changed man.

THE NEW CALIGULA

൪

Almost immediately, Caligula began to behave in irrational and violent ways. He became convinced that his illness was the result of poison, and that his erstwhile co-regent Tiberius Gemellus had conspired to kill him. He ordered Gamellus to be murdered without a trial. When his grandmother Antonia, who was also Gamellus' grandmother, objected to this action, he murdered her, too.

൪

HE AND HIS favorite sister Julia Drusilla, whom he had named as his heir while he was ill, began a torrid incestuous relationship. He was jealously obsessed with her. Despite the fact that she had already married a man named Marcus Aemilius Lepidus, Caligula took her away from her husband and kept her with him in the palace as his wife. He also indulged in a sexual relationship with another sister, Julia Livilla, who was a frequent participant in the orgies that he hosted. He lavished these two sisters with honors, gifts and favors far in excess of anything that Roman society had seen or allowed before.

※

THE REST of his family did not fare as well. He had his brother-in-law killed, and he forced his father-in-law to slit his own throat. The only blood relation who survived his rages was Claudius, his uncle, who was deaf in one ear and had a limp as a result of a childhood illness. Caligula enjoyed using Claudius as a whipping boy and the butt of jokes, and for this reason, Claudius had value to the young and unstable emperor.

※

HIS WIVES SUFFERED, as well. His first wife, Junia, was the most unscathed thanks to her early death. His second wife was Livia Orestilla, whom he stole from her wedding to Caius Piso. He ordered her taken from her wedding feast and put into his house, where he abused her for two days before "divorcing" her. She was later exiled for returning to Piso, the man she had intended to marry in the first place.

※

AFTER THIS, he summoned Lollia Paulina away from her husband, Publius Memmius Regulus, the governor of Macedonia. He had heard that her grandmother had been a beautiful woman and that Lollia had inherited that beauty, and he wanted to see her for himself. When she arrived in Rome for her royal audience, he married her against her will. He cast her off not long after, but he decreed that she would never be allowed to have any relationship of any kind with any man thereafter.

※

HIS NATURAL TENDENCIES continued to assert themselves, and he insisted upon being addressed as "Dutiful", "The Pious," and "the Greatest and Best Caesar." He wanted to name himself king, but upon being told that he was above the grandeur of all other princes and kings, he decided that he was a god instead. He said,

※

"I have existed from the morning of the world and I shall exist until the last star falls from the night. I am all men as I am no man and therefore I am a god."

※

HE ORDERED statues of all of the gods to be deprived of their heads, and to have his own likeness put on them instead. He suffered manic mood swings and was overheard shouting at Jupiter,

"If you don't cast me up to heaven, I will cast you down to hell!"

He invited the goddess Luna to come to his bed during the full moon and fully believed that he was making love to her. He began to force people to worship him with prayers and sacrifices, and he demanded to be addressed as the king of the Roman gods. He hand-picked the clergy in his new cult of self-obsession and often attended the rituals in person so he could receive the adoration directly. To complete his transformation from human to god, he had extensions built that connected his palace to the temples so that his home and the gods' homes were the same.

※

WHEN HIS BELOVED sister and lover Drusilla died suddenly of fever in 39 AD, he fell into deep grief. He kept her body with him in his chambers for four days before his friends were able to convince him to give her over to the temple for burial. He stopped trimming his hair and beard, and he banned everyone in the empire from bathing, laughing, or even dining with their families. He proclaimed Drusilla a deity and required people to swear oaths in her name, and he put a statue of his sister in the temple of Venus. His obsession with her continued for the rest of his life.

BLOODSHED AND BRUTALITY

※

In late 38 or early 39, a famine struck Rome. The emperor's response was to expand and improve the port, allowing greater shipments of grain to be brought in from Egypt. He built and improved roads, temples and public buildings throughout the empire.

※

HIS GENEROSITY and good management ended there. He depleted the empire's coffers by building extravagant pleasure boats, allegedly even plating the decks with gold. He hosted floating banquets on Lake Nemi, attended by friends and political foes alike. On one occasion, at the end of the banquet, he had all of his guests thrown overboard.

※

CALIGULA TURNED his attention to the military, organizing a

campaign into Germania and beyond. He reached as far as the English Channel, but his men refused to cross due to the weather and the approaching winter season. Unwilling to return to Rome without a victory, Caligula ordered his men to wade into the water and fight the waves. The army gathered a mountain of seashells on the emperor's orders, and they were used to build a lighthouse on the shore. He then paid all of the soldiers 400 sesterces, telling them, "Go your way happy; go your way rich."

HE RETURNED to Rome to find that his extravagance and botched military adventures had left the treasury virtually empty. To assuage this situation, he pursued several different strategies. He seized the property of his exiled sisters and auctioned everything to the rich provincials in Gaul. He accused many rich *equites* and members of the Senatorial class of crimes, most of which were imaginary, and upon their inevitable conviction he appropriated their property and riches. Caligula also sharply raised taxes, imposing levies on everything he could think of, including the sex acts performed in Roman brothels. He even began to tax sexual acts between husbands and their wives.

CALIGULA'S FONDNESS for brothels was so great that he turned one wing of his own palace into a whorehouse, and he forced the wives, daughters and young sons of the aristocracy to work there. His functionaries kept careful records of who came to visit and what services they received. Those who came to patronize the brothel were charged exorbitant amounts of money, and if they couldn't afford the fee, they were granted loans with interest. The emperor called the unfortunate and unwilling denizens of the brothel "contributors to the Imperial Revenue."

His depravity began to exert itself with ever crueler and more creative humiliations for the Senatorial class, who had become the primary target for his ire. He would go for long rides in his carriage, forcing patricians to run alongside him in their togas. He would invite married couples to dine with him, and during the meal he would take the wives into another room and rape them. He would then return his victim to her husband, and over the remainder of the dinner, the emperor would comment on the woman's sexual skills. He forced Senators to kneel at his feet while he ate and to serve him like slaves, even compelling them to dress in the short linen tunics that slaves wore.

He loved public spectacles, gladiatorial combat and chariot races. He trained with gladiators using real weapons instead of the wooden practice swords that were meant to be used. He killed a hapless sparring partner and declared himself a gladiatorial champion. He was an avid supporter of certain gladiators and chariot racing teams, and when the crowds would cheer for someone other than his darlings, he would fly into a rage. On these occasions, he would remove the awnings that shaded the crowd. If anyone dared to leave their seats to seek shelter, they were arrested and executed for insulting the emperor. When meat became scarce and the wild beasts used in the arena were in danger of going unfed, Caligula had criminals thrown to the animals instead, no matter how minor their infractions had been.

On one occasion, when there were no more slaves available to be killed and the wild beasts were still hungry, Caligula had his soldiers take an entire section of onlookers from their seats and force them into the arena. He later said that his reason for doing this was that he was bored.

Caligula's behavior toward his people was becoming more and more erratic. He paid for elaborate theatrical performances and let it be known that the seats would be free. When people arrived to take advantage of the offer, they were driven away with clubs. In one such episode, several members of the knightly class and their ladies were trampled to death in the ensuing panic.

His hatred for the Senatorial class knew no bounds, it seemed. He would have aristocrats branded on the face, or he would send them to work in the mines in appalling conditions. He forced some patricians to fight in the arena, usually to face lions and bears, and if they did not entertain him sufficiently with their performances, he would have them bound into cages on their hands and knees. When he tired of seeing them this way, he would have them sawed in half.

CALIGULA WAS KNOWN to pray for disasters. He wanted famine, plagues, massacres, earthquakes, volcanic eruptions – anything that would cause a dreadful loss of life. His reasoning for this was that history only remembers tragedies, and he wanted to be remembered. It seems that he got his wish.

HIS CAPRICIOUS CRUELTY found an extreme outlet at one banquet. When he was told that a slave had been caught stealing silver, he had the man's hands cut off and tied around his neck along with a sign proclaiming his crime. The unfortunate slave was then forced to parade around the room, telling dinner guests what he had done. He bled to death before he completed his rounds.

DEATH AND EXECUTION BECAME COMMONPLACE, and there were many reasons why the emperor condemned his subjects. He would have people killed for looking at him, for not looking at him, for forgetting his birthday, for writing music he didn't like, or for not complimenting him. He was said to be losing his hair, so he would kill men who sat above him and saw his bald spot, and if someone had better hair than him, he would have them executed for spite. He would force parents to watch while their children were executed, and he would joke with them during their ordeal. Caligula called these random and seemingly senseless killings "clearing his accounts."

THE EMPEROR MARRIED AGAIN in the summer of the year 39, this time to a woman named Milonia Caesonia. At the time of their marriage, she had already borne three children to other men and was heavily pregnant. She had a reputation for indiscriminate promiscuity and was accused in some quarters of being a prostitute. She was the love of Caligula's life. Caesonia gave birth to a daughter shortly after their wedding, and the child was named Julia Drusilla in honor of his beloved sister. He claimed the child as his own and cited her vicious temper as proof of his paternity. Caesonia and Caligula were alike in their prodigious and unnatural sexual proclivities. They both flaunted their sex lives with males and females. He would strip his new wife in the presence of his friends, displaying her for them. When he would review his troops, she would ride with him, dressed in full military regalia. He was so enamored of her that he once threatened to torture her to make her reveal why she had such a hold on him. This never came to fruition, luckily for Caesonia.

ONE OF HIS most extreme spending sprees allegedly caused a famine in Rome as a result of the emperor suspending grain deliveries so that the carts could be used in the construction of his project. In the summer of the year 40, he ordered a bridge to be constructed between the ports of Puteoli and Bauli on the Gulf of Baiae. The bridge was nearly three miles long, and it was made of two rows of grain ships, tethered together and buried under dirt to make an approximation of a road. When the bridge was completed, Caligula donned a breast plate that had supposedly belonged to Alexander the Great, along with a purple cloak and jewels from India, and he rode his favorite horse Incitatus, whom Caligula later made a senator, the entire length of the bridge. He was accompanied by cavalry and infantry, and when they reached the end of the bridge, they stormed Puteoli as if it was an enemy encampment and they were bent upon conquering it.

THE NEXT DAY, he and his army rode back to Bauli. The entire procession was performed in the manner of a military triumph. He had carts full of treasures and loot that he had taken in Germania, and he marched a Parthian prince as a captive. He was followed by his soldiers and cavalry, and this time he was accompanied by members of the aristocracy who had been pressed into participation. When the parade reached the center of the bridge, a stage was erected, and there the emperor gave a lengthy speech praising his soldiers but mostly raving about himself. A banquet was held on the bridge, complete with bonfires. Cassius Dio wrote that at the end of the party,

> "he hurled many of his companions off the bridge into the sea and sank many of the others by sailing about and attacking them in boats equipped with beaks. Some perished, but the majority, though drunk managed to save themselves."

AFTER THIS EVENT, Caligula boasted that he had been able to ride a horse across the sea, and that this made him greater than Alexander the Great and King Xerxes combined.

Suetonius, Josephus and Cassius Dio all allege that because Caligula had commandeered ships and carts, grain supplies were unable to reach the people of Rome. The interruption of the delivery of foodstuffs caused a famine in the city and was more proof of the emperor's insanity and instability.

※

It was during this period, when he was ordering the construction of temples and statues where he could be worshipped, that he showed a complete lack of understanding of some of the finer points of running a multicultural empire. Rome at that time was in command of the Middle East, specifically Judea and the city of Jerusalem. Caligula ordered that a huge statue of himself be erected in the Temple on the Mount, the holiest site of the Jewish faith. Josephus, the Jewish historian who was a contemporary of Caligula, recorded that this move, which was considered tantamount to desecration, caused violent unrest in Jerusalem. The failure of the Jews to properly venerate the emperor was seen as a rebellion against the authority of Rome, and the perceived disloyalty was handled very harshly, almost to the point of civil war. Caligula was convinced to remove the statue by his friend Julius Agrippa, the king of Judea. From then on, Caligula had a very negative opinion of the Jews, and the historian Philo wrote that he

> "regarded the Jews with most especial suspicion, as if they were the only persons who cherished wishes opposed to his."

PLOTS AND SCHEMES

༺༻

Throughout his life, Caligula was the target of multiple conspiracies and assassination attempts. The frequency with which he was betrayed almost excuses the level of paranoia that he exhibited. It's said that Praetorian Macro, the man whose influence over Tiberius led to Caligula's inheritance, rescued him from many attempts on his life while he was living on Capri. He was anticipated to be Tiberius's heir long before he was named as such, and many people felt that they would be better served if he was out of the way.

༺༻

THE FIRST CONSPIRACY against him once he became emperor took place when he was in the grips of his mystery ailment. Macro and his own father-in-law, Silanus, began preparations for Tiberius Gamellus to take the throne. They intended to use Gamellus to full advantage, capitalizing on his loyalty to them in return for having him named emperor. Macro's wife, Ennia, Caligula's sometimes lover, was also involved. All three were scheming for a way to use Caligula's imminent demise to their own advantage. When he was well, the emperor learned of their plans, and that was the end of them. Gamellus also paid the price in full for being the presumptive next emperor, and a centurion and a tribune were sent to help him commit suicide.

※

WHILE HE WAS ILL, as already mentioned, he had named his beloved sister Julia Drusilla his heir in all things. In practice, this meant that her husband, Marcus Aemilius Lepidus, would be the next emperor, for no females were permitted to rule in Rome. Lepidus was well pleased with this impending honor. When Drusilla died, however, his hopes were dashed. He allied himself with Caligula's sisters, Agrippina the Younger and Julia Livilla. Their treachery came to light while Caligula was on campaign in Germania. Lepidus was executed. His sisters were punished and sent into exile after being humiliated publicly by being forced to have sex with his friends, freedmen and slaves.

※

ANOTHER CONSPIRACY, one of which we have virtually no details. Several high-ranking senators were apparently charged with treason, and many of them were executed. Some sources claim as much as fifty percent of the Senate were slain in the resulting purge. Those senators who survived the purge resolved to offer sacrifices to the gods in honor of his mercy.

V
A VERY UN-ROMAN EMPEROR

Would that the Roman people had but one neck!
Caligula

Caligula became more and more estranged from the people of Rome, and he systematically destroyed more than half of the 600 men who sat in the Senate, either literally or figuratively. Like his predecessor Tiberius, he began to withdraw from public life, retreating further and further into his delusions. He released his strangle hold on power, and in the process, he made one mistake too many.

A HELLENISTIC EDUCATION

❧

As the son of a royal line, Caligula was provided with the greatest education available at the time. He was tutored extensively by Greek slaves, learning philosophy and rhetoric as well as history. He was fascinated by Alexander the Great and his father Xerxes, and as earlier stated, he possessed a breastplate and shield that supposedly belonged to the great man and were said to have been taken from Alexander's grave.

❧

AS HIS DISSATISFACTION with Rome increased, his interest in the eastern half of the empire grew. In his childhood, he had accompanied his father to Syria and Egypt. He liked the eastern way of doing things. Rome had expunged monarchy during the Republic, believing (perhaps correctly) that it was too prone to corruption to be trusted. In the east, there were no such reservations. Kings and autocrats were a solid and ancient feature of the region, and Caligula liked the way that sounded.

※

Two of his personal friends were vassal kings that he met during his childhood when he was living at his grandmother Antonia's estate. King Julius Agrippa of Judea and King Antiochus IV of Commagene (a kingdom located in modern-day Armenia) were in his entourage, and the two were referred to in whispers as Caligula's "tyrant-trainers". They encouraged his intention to overturn the falsehood of pseudo-democracy that Augustus had instituted with the Senate. He planned to dissolve the Senate and declare himself king in the autocratic style of the east.

※

Caligula began plans to move the capital from Rome to Alexandria. Moving the locus of power would mean that the Senate, which was already virtually impotent, would lose the rest of its prestige. They would no longer be able to exercise their flattery and influence trading, and the Senate would become essentially obsolete.

※

It was too much. The Senate had already borne the brunt of his misdeeds and wanton cruelty. They were ready to be rid of him.

ENOUGH IS ENOUGH

❦

Caligula was protected by two sets of bodyguards: The Praetorians, including tribunes Cassius Chaerea and Cornelius Sabinus, and a group of Germanic mercenaries who were loyal to the emperor alone. As Caligula continued his purges of the Senatorial class, he turned to Chaerea and his men to do his dirty work. Torture, murder and arbitrary summary executions were all carried out by the Praetorians. The emperor enjoyed having the Praetorian guard, the special forces unit of their day, perform their training exercises in public, a veiled reminder to the population of Rome that these lethal men were under his command.

❦

HATRED for Caligula begat hatred for the Praetorian guard, and Chaerea began to worry that if something happened to the emperor, he would be swept away with him. Already there had been multiple conspiracies and attempts on Caligula's life, and it was virtually a foregone conclusion that a life led with such violence would eventually end the same way. Chaerea was justified in his fears.

※

THE SENATE KNEW of his concerns, and they capitalized on them. Some of the more powerful senators met with him in secret, telling him that he would indeed be the focus of the people's wrath when Caligula was finally assassinated. Wouldn't it be better for him when the time came, they reasoned, if it was his hand on the knife?

※

CHAEREA WAS MORE than amenable to the suggestion. As a member of the Praetorians, he had access to Caligula in his most unguarded moments, and every day presented him with multiple opportunities to strike. Along with his concerns for his own longevity if the emperor should fall, he hated Caligula on a personal level. Caligula often mocked him, accusing him of a lack of manhood and belittling him due to his high-pitched voice. Chaerea had been publicly humiliated by the emperor on more than one occasion, and he burned with hatred for Caligula.

※

AFTER BEING TAPPED as the intended assassin, Chaerea would have gone immediately to perform the task, but the senators wanted him to wait until they had a successor in place. They wanted to avoid the chaos of an empty throne.

※

CALIGULA

So Chaerea waited, and the Senate, as the Senate was wont to do, debated. Part of that august body wanted to abolish the Principate (the rule of the emperor) and re-establish the Republic. Another group wanted to name a new emperor, one who would be beholden to the Senate for his good fortune. Both sides believed that they had much to gain personally from a shake-up in the halls of power, and they resolved to milk the situation for as much benefit as they could.

※

The debate went on for days, maybe even weeks. Finally, the Republicans lost the fight and attention turned to selecting Caligula's successor. The only surviving member of the Julio-Claudian dynasty who could inherit was Caligula's uncle, Claudius, who, as stated earlier, had been kept alive because of his value as a laughing stock. He was an uninspiring choice for emperor, and many people felt that his unfitness for the job was self-evident. Ultimately, it was decided that this very unfitness was the perfect condition for an imperial puppet. The Senate decided that Claudius would be the next emperor, and Chaerea was given the go-ahead.

※

In the first weeks of the year 41, Caligula was absorbed in arranging for a new set of theatrical performances intended to honor the memory of the deified Augustus. The emperor and his retinue were walking through an underground passage beneath the theater when they encountered a group of actors rehearsing for the coming performance. Chaerea and Sabinus were with Caligula, along with other guards and his usual hangers-on. Chaerea ordered the Germanic guards to continue escorting the emperor's companions to their seats, and they stayed with Caligula while he stopped to chat with the actors.

❦

As soon as the Germanic guards and their charges were gone, Chaerea drew his sword and struck Caligula in the neck. Almost simultaneously, Sabinus stabbed him in the chest. The emperor fell, but shouted that he was still alive. The rest of the Praetorians fell on him with their blades, and he was stabbed more than thirty times. As historian Cassius Dio wrote,

> "Caligula learned by actual experience that he was not a god."

❦

The Praetorians then swept into the palace and murdered the empress Caesonia, stabbing her to death. Little Julia Drusilla was seized by the ankles and had her brains dashed out against a wall.

❦

Caligula was dead. The nightmare was over.

AFTERMATH

❧

Rome exploded into chaos upon the news that the tyrant was dead. In the confusion, the Praetorians seized Claudius and bundled him off to their camp, where they proclaimed him *imperator*. Caligula's Germanic bodyguards went berserk, combing the city for conspirators and killing virtually anyone they felt they could suspect. They murdered a number of innocent people before they were finally stopped.

❧

THE SENATE ACCLAIMED Claudius after another brief debate, and he was given imperial honors the next day. The people of Rome, who had not suffered as much as the nobles under Caligula's rule and still supported him, flooded into the Forum and demanded the deaths of the conspirators. The Senate was happy to comply. They arrested and executed

Chaerea for doing what they asked him to do, and Sabinus, rather than suffer the same fate, committed suicide.

VI
IT'S ALL TRUE...OR IS IT?

I scorn their hatred, if they do but fear me
Caligula

⁂

Everything you've just read is the history and reputation of Caligula that's been handed down for centuries. Thanks to the writings of historians like Suetonius, Tacitus, Philo, Seneca, Cassius Dio and Josephus, Caligula's excesses are almost common knowledge. But what if the accepted wisdom is wrong?

CONTRADICTIONS AND INCONSISTENCIES

❧

In his book *Caligula: A Biography*, Aloys Winterling takes a different approach to the emperor's legends. He argues convincingly that Caligula is the subject of a smear campaign that has lasted for centuries.

❧

THE BASIS of his argument is a number of inconsistencies within the writings of the historians listed above, especially Suetonius. The historians present tales of Caligula's insanity, but in practically the same paragraph, they describe him behaving in a very deliberate and rational way. Winterling posits that Caligula was not mad at all. He suggests that the emperor was retaliating against the Senatorial class for their duplicity, favor peddling and treachery.

❧

During Caligula's youth, he saw how the members of the Senate betrayed one another in search of favor and career advancement. The atmosphere in Rome was one of fear, denunciation, accusation, and false flattery. The least critical comment about the emperor would be used as the basis for accusations of treason, and Tiberius' prisons were full to groaning with people whose friends had reported them for impolitic statements.

※

In Winterling's interpretation, when Caligula became emperor, he was subjected to flattery of the most duplicitous kind. Senators and the aristocratic elite said whatever they thought he wanted to hear. He took this as an affront and felt, not without justification, that he was being lied to.

※

It was the scheming and back-stabbing of the aristocracy that had led to the deaths of his parents and older brothers. He himself had been subject to attempts by the senatorial class to draw him into openly criticizing Tiberius while he was still residing on Capri. He saw them as the enemy, and his actions were all designed to ruin the senatorial class by means of their own hypocrisy.

※

When Caligula suffered his mysterious, near-fatal illness early in his reign, members of the Senate and aristocracy took to grandstanding and making public oaths regarding what they would do if the gods spared the emperor's life. Their oaths were less about concern for Caligula's wellbeing than about presenting a pious and loyal face for the crowd. By being showy and loud in their supposed loyalty to the emperor, they hoped to curry favor.

※

Two men learned the hard way that the emperor was going to hold everyone to their word. While Caligula was lingering near death, a man named Afranius Potitus publicly offered to give up his life if only the emperor would live. Another man, Atanius Secundus, swore that he would go into the arena as a gladiator if Caligula recovered. When the emperor regained his health and heard of these oaths, he pressed these men to hold up their ends of the bargain. Otherwise, the reasoning went, they would be proven to be liars. Faced with losing all of the standing they already had, and without gaining the favor that they'd hoped to earn, both men reluctantly and fatally kept their promises.

※

Winterling uses sources outside the accepted histories to examine several of the more outrageous claims made against Caligula. He discredits almost all of them. The assertion that young Caligula spent time frequenting brothels and taverns while residing on Capri is made only by Suetonius. There is no evidence, either in the historical record or archaeologically, that any brothels or temples ever existed on the island. Further, that exact behavior was also ascribed to the emperor Nero, and in that case, it was probably true.

ANOTHER OF THE more infamous claims made by Suetonius and others is that Caligula turned one wing of his palace into a brothel staffed by married women and young boys who were conscripted against their will. However, historian Cassius Dio states that these were in fact the wives and children of the consular class, and that they were being "hosted" by Caligula at an exorbitant cost.

※

WINTERLING WRITES,

> "relationships between the emperor and the aristocracy continued to be expressed in the old ceremonies of friendship, morning receptions, evening banquets, reciprocal support in financial matters, and testamentary bequests."

This means that in order to prove that they were friends with the emperor, the nobles had to reciprocate all of the gifts he gave them. He demanded huge outlays of gold and silver to support these "guests" in his home, and there was no politically expedient way for the nobles to object. To do so would be to reject the emperor's friendship, which would lead to denunciation by other nobles who were trying to get on Caligula's good side by turning on his perceived enemies. They did not understand that they were all his enemies.

※

CALIGULA'S SELF-DEIFICATION is another point where

Winterling finds inconsistencies, and another interpretation. It was, in fact, not unusual for emperors to be deified and worshipped as gods. Augustus had been added to the Roman pantheon upon his death, and god-kings had existed for centuries in the eastern reaches of the empire. The idea of worshipping the emperor as a god was nothing new. The difference in Caligula's case is that he didn't wait until he died to be made a god. Once he had a temple built in his own honor, Suetonius writes,

> "The richest citizens used all their influence to secure the priesthoods of his cult and to bid high for the honor."

※

CALIGULA'S INTENT was to bleed the noble houses dry, to force them to ruin themselves in pursuit of favor he was disinclined to ever give. His every move, every "mad" act, was designed to mock and belittle the aristocratic culture of favor for favor and toadyism. This was especially true of his most infamous act: appointing a horse to the Senate.

※

CALIGULA HAD A FAVORITE HORSE, Incitatus (which means "hot spur"). He invited his horse to attend a banquet, where he lavished luxuries and praise on the animal and discussed his intention to make Incitatus a consul. He built a palace for the horse, staffed it completely, and included a dining hall so that people could be invited to dinners. In Winterling's interpretation, this was not done out of any sort of mania or insanity. It was a long, theatrical mockery of the ambitions of the senatorial class, equating them to a horse. Through his display, he was utterly devaluing the aristocracy.

POISON PENS

༺❦༻

If Winterling's theory is true, and if Caligula was not insane at all, then why would these historians want to damage his memory and treat him so unfairly?

༺❦༻

OF ALL OF the historians who wrote about Caligula, only Josephus actually met the emperor in the flesh. His stories of the emperor are colored with the anger left over from conflicts in Jerusalem between the Romans and the Jews, and his impartiality is suspect. Cassius Dio was a contemporary of the emperor, and his writings are largely void of the most sensational stories of depravity. Suetonius was writing about Caligula fully a hundred years after the emperor's death, and it appears that he based his work on earlier sources, but he distorted events that had been recorded, or he took them out of context entirely.

A WRITER in Rome needed to stay on the good side of the Senate. Historians and even playwrights could be and often were banished because they wrote something that cast some powerful person in a bad light. The reigns of Caligula and of Tiberius before him were marked by the worst sort of sycophantic behavior by the Senate. When Suetonius was writing a century after these tumultuous events, the Senate wanted to present an image of serenity and wisdom. Having the sins of earlier incarnations of their assembly would have been embarrassing. Winterling writes,

> "A frank account of past events documented not only the emperor's despotism but also the unscrupulous opportunism of some senators and the submissiveness of the Senate as a whole – discreditable behavior which the Senate would have preferred forgotten."

SUETONIUS, in fact, is the first person to ever accuse Caligula of being insane. This, too, fell in line with the goals and aims of his time. He wrote while the emperor and the Senate were enjoying a period of détente, where the shadows of autocracy were no longer falling on the face of Rome. It was much more politically expedient, not to mention more satisfying, to take an emperor who truly exercised imperial power and label him as insane. Only a madman would be such a tyrant, the thinking went, and only madmen would support such a system of rule. After years of civil unrest and bloodshed, anything that could cast unrestrained imperial power in a bad light was welcome and necessary to help keep the peace.

※

FROM SUETONIUS ONWARD, it was all just repetition. Scholars depended upon his history of the Caesars and based their own biographies and writings on his words. Inevitably, the image of a deranged and murderous emperor crept into the world's consciousness, and Caligula's name and reputation were permanently tarnished.

❦ VII ❧
LESSONS TO LEARN

❦

So, what are lessons are we to take from the life of Caligula? It depends upon which version of story you believe is true. Whether he was the brutal madman that Suetonius describes, or if he was the ruthless but rational emperor shown by Winterling, there are certain elements of his character that remain consistent.

BELIEVE IT OR NOT, HE HAD GOOD QUALITIES

༺༻

The quality that Caligula can most be praised for is his intelligence. Even his detractors, like Josephus, credited him with being a talented orator and a learned man. He was fluent in Greek and could quote philosophy and epic poetry with facility. Apart from his formal education, Caligula was also astute enough to read the people around him and know how to keep himself alive during the dangerous days on Capri. He learned from his uncle's mistakes and seemed to be on track to doing all the right things as emperor, at least until his illness.

༺༻

IN THE DAYS before his life-changing illness, he was loyal to his family, especially to the three sisters who had been at his side during the maelstrom of trauma following Germanicus's death. Caligula, Drusilla, Agrippina and Livilla were united in their efforts to survive in the aftermath of the treason convictions of their mother and brothers. His sisters were accorded the highest honors he could give upon his ascension to the throne, and had he not become ill, and had the two youngest not decided to cast their lots with Lepidus instead of remaining loyal to him, he would have continued to be a devoted brother.

PERHAPS BECAUSE HE had been shown so little of it, he respected loyalty in others. Both Cassius Dio and Josephus wrote of a time when a senator named Pomponius was accused of treason by his "friend," Timid us. At the time, Pomponius was having an affair with a beautiful actress named Quintilia. She was seized by the Praetorians and tortured so brutally by Chaerea that she was permanently disfigured. Despite her suffering, she never betrayed any confidences, and she refused to say whether Pomponius was or was not involved in any plans against the emperor. She was brought before Caligula, and he was so moved by her strength and nobility in resisting extreme pressure to renounce her lover that he had Pomponius released, and he provided Quintilia with 800,000 sesterces as a gift.

ANOTHER QUALITY, and a surprising one, is that he had a strangely populist bent. He made changes in the law that permitted slaves to bring complaints against their masters and to testify against them during trials. He also counted among his closest friends a pair of freedmen, men who had once been slaves themselves. These freedmen were with him throughout his life, and in fact they were part of the entourage that was ushered away from the emperor on the night he met his end. Even if all of the stories of his excesses are true, he focused his wrath on the aristocracy instead of the common man, and he continually provided the people with food and entertainment.

FAMOUS FOR BAD BEHAVIOR

※

His bad points almost don't need to be enumerated. Assuming for just a moment that his behavior after his illness was an aberration, or that the stories told about him were untrue, he still had certain character defects that we can point to with certainty.

※

Not surprisingly for someone born into a royal family, he was arrogant and self-centered. He was saddled with a horrid temper – remember, it was Julia Drusilla the Younger's vicious temper that convinced him that she was his biological daughter. Perhaps we can add self-awareness to his list of good traits.

※

HIS SEXUAL PROCLIVITIES WERE QUESTIONABLE, and when he chose a partner, he often had little interest in whether or not she (or he) consented to his attentions. Again, if the stories are to be believed, he also had a long history of committing incest with his sisters.

※

ANOTHER OF HIS bad qualities was that he was vindictive. Again, even if we accept Winterling's thesis, Caligula was unable to let go of his hatred for the Senate and the aristocratic classes of Rome. He had an almost insatiable desire for revenge and his need to punish the nobility went beyond reason. Had he been a little less bent on destroying the Senators and the entire noble class, his reign might have lasted longer than three years, and he might have lived to see his thirtieth birthday.

※

HE WAS immoderate in his tastes. He spent money like it was going out of style, depleting the over-stuffed Roman treasury left to him by Tiberius in less than a year. He would bathe daily in expensive oils. He had the habit of drinking vinegar in which priceless pearls had been dissolved, and his second wife Lollia Paulina once made a public appearance wearing jewelry valued at more than forty million sesterces. Profligacy was apparently a family trait.

※

MANY PEOPLE in ancient Rome loved the spectacle of the arena, but Caligula was more devoted than most. He wined and dined chariot drivers, actors and other performers, and the mime Mnester spent so much time in the emperor's private company that rumors flew about a homosexual love affair. He was young, with a young man's tastes, which were considered beneath the dignity of his station.

LESSONS TO BE LEARNED

❦

Of all the lessons to be learned from studying Caligula, perhaps the most obvious is that there is profound danger in autocracy. As the adage states, absolute power corrupts absolutely, and there was no power more absolute than that held by the Roman emperors. With no checks in place, they were free to do whatever they pleased, to whomever they pleased, without fear of reprisal. When your word is law, laws no longer matter. As Caligula himself once said, "All things are lawful for me."

❦

IN AUTOCRACY, danger exists in the behavior of the average citizen, as well. People turn on one another, even on their friends, to save their own necks when fear and denunciation are the flavor of the week. Under an autocratic government the only way a person can ensure that he and his immediate family will be spared from the hangman's noose is by betraying an innocent friend. People who otherwise would have no ill will toward one another become complicit in the excesses of the ruling elite.

※

ANOTHER MORE PERSONAL lesson is taught by those around Caligula as well as by the emperor himself. It's all right to be ambitious, but it's best to keep those ambitions within reason. People like Sejanus and Lepidus were saddled with aspirations that were too high for them to safely reach without resorting to murder and deceit. Caligula's hope to establish an eastern style monarchy to the detriment of the Senate was his undoing. Reaching too high can have disastrous consequences.

※

ON A MORE POSITIVE NOTE, Caligula's ability to read social cues and his understanding of his precarious situation on Capri can be an inspiration for us to stay aware of things going on around us in our own lives. If we go through life oblivious to the intentions of other people, we stand the chance of being caught in some very nasty surprises. If Caligula had been less aware of the consequences of speaking freely, or if he hadn't been able to read the intentions of the people trying to draw him into incriminating himself, he would not have survived to adulthood.

※

THE DISPARITY BETWEEN DIFFERENT HISTORIANS' accounts can teach us the value of critical thinking. We can't believe everything we're told. Most writers have a bias in their work, although few are as blatant as Suetonius. Bias can lead to fabrication and the death of truth. In highly politicized and fractious times, ignorance of bias can be deadly. Belief in falsehoods can easily turn into unjustified actions, which can in turn lead to devastating repercussions.

༺☙༻

THE BEST LESSON that can be learned from Caligula's story, and from the presentation of that story after his death, is this: choose your enemies carefully. What they have to say will live longer than you, and will probably be believed. Just look at the damage to Caligula's reputation and legacy thanks to Suetonius and his friends and patrons in the Senate.

AFTERWORD

Caligula remains one of the most infamous of Roman emperors. We have presented both interpretations of the events of his reign. Either he was a madman, a murderer and a nightmare of a human being, or he was a rational but vindictive ruler with an axe to grind. No matter what the truth was – and it may well have been between those two extremes – the fact is that Caligula will maintain his place in the public psyche for many years to come.

ADDITIONAL READING

Additional Reading

Consider these texts if you would like to read even more about Caligula:

Annals, by Tacitus, © 2012 Acheron Press.

Legends of the Ancient World: The Life and Legacy of Caligula, by Charles River Editors, © 2013, Charles River Editors, Boston, Massachusetts, USA.

Caius Caesar Caligula: The Lives of the Twelve Caesars, Vol. IV, by Gaius Suetonius Tranquilius, © 2015 SMK Books, Floyd, Virginia, USA.

Caligula: A Biography, by Aloys Winterling, translated by Deborah Lucas Schneider, Glenn W. Most and Paul Psoinos, © 2011 University of California Press, Ltd., Los Angeles, California.

ADDITIONAL READING

Caligula: The Evil Emperor Who Declared Himself a God, by D. M. Alon, © 2013 by Doron Alon and Numinosity Press, Inc., New York, New York, USA.

Caligula: A Life from Beginning to End, by Hourly History, © 2017, Hourly History Limited, New York, USA.

YOUR FREE EBOOK!

As a way of saying thank you for reading our book, we're offering you a free copy of the below eBook.

Happy Reading!

GO WWW.THEHISTORYHOUR.COM/CLEO/

Printed in Great Britain
by Amazon